Mammals
of the Sea

WELDON OWEN PTY LTD
Chairman: John Owen
Publisher: Sheena Coupe
Associate Publisher: Lynn Humphries
Managing Editor: Helen Bateman
Design Concept: Sue Rawkins
Senior Designer: Kylie Mulquin
Production Manager: Caroline Webber
Production Assistant: Kylie Lawson

Text: Robert Coupe
Consultant: Craig Sowden, Curator, Sydney Aquarium
U.S. Editors: Laura Cavaluzzo and Rebecca McEwen

06 05 04 03 02
10 9 8 7 6 5 4

Published in the United States by
Wright Group/McGraw-Hill
19201 120th Avenue NE, Suite 100
Bothell, WA 98011
www.WrightGroup.com

Printed in Singapore.
ISBN: 0-7699-0470-X

CONTENTS

WHAT IS A WHALE?

Like humans, whales are mammals. Unlike humans, whales live in the sea. There are many different kinds of whales. The blue whale is the largest animal on Earth. Other whales are quite small. Dolphins and porpoises are also kinds of whales.

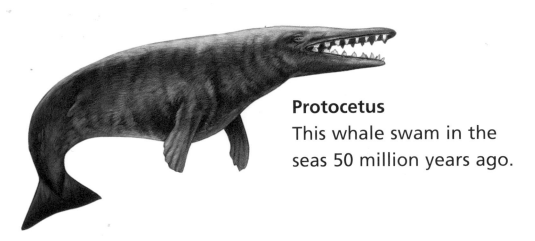

Protocetus
This whale swam in the seas 50 million years ago.

Mesonyx
This land mammal is believed by some scientists to be the ancestor of the whale.

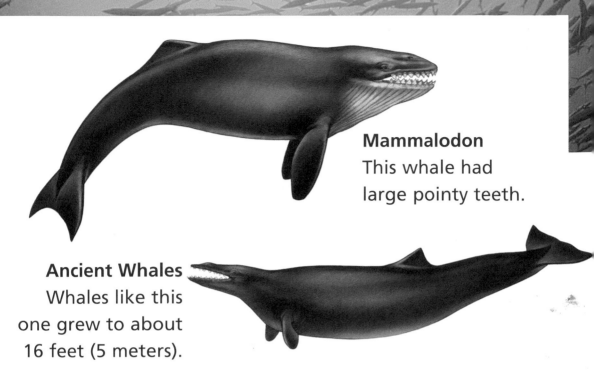

Mammalodon
This whale had large pointy teeth.

Ancient Whales
Whales like this one grew to about 16 feet (5 meters).

DID YOU KNOW?

Moby Dick is the name of the whale in one of the most famous whale stories ever written.

TEETH OR NO TEETH

Some types of whales have teeth and some do not. Whales with teeth are called toothed whales. They mainly eat fish. Whales with no teeth are called baleen whales. They have long strands called baleen hanging from their upper jaw. They strain sea water through these strands and eat tiny fish and shrimp.

BALEEN WHALE

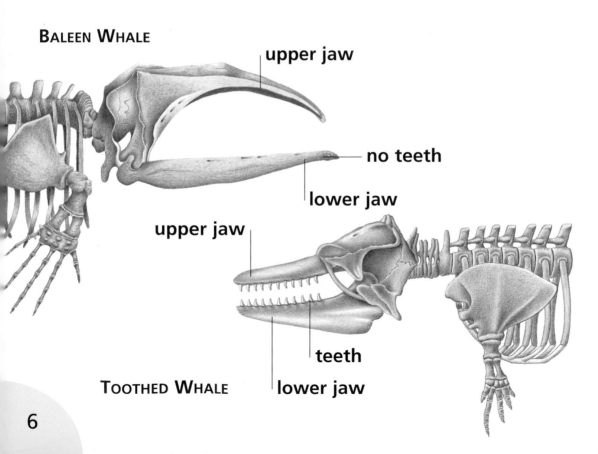

upper jaw

no teeth

lower jaw

upper jaw

teeth

TOOTHED WHALE   lower jaw

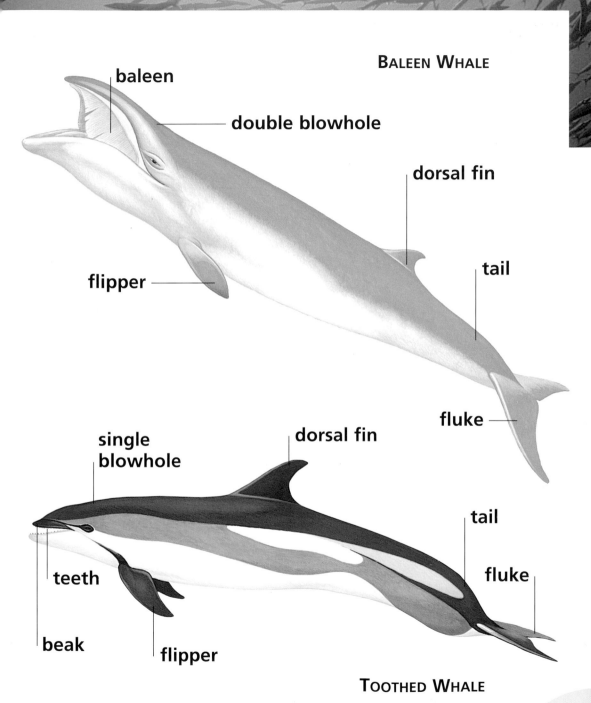

BALEEN WHALE

baleen

double blowhole

dorsal fin

tail

flipper

fluke

single blowhole

dorsal fin

tail

fluke

teeth

beak

flipper

TOOTHED WHALE

7

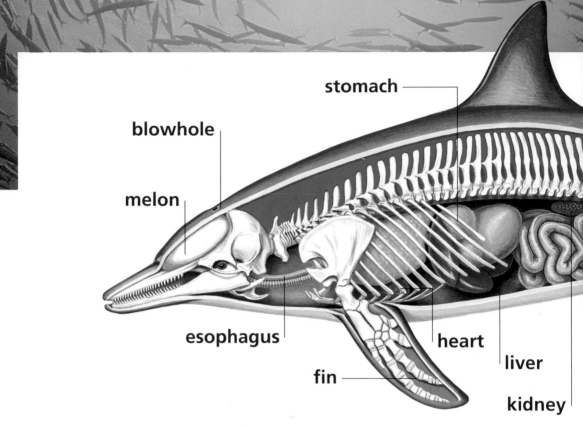

stomach

blowhole

melon

esophagus

fin

heart

liver

kidney

LOOKING INSIDE

A whale has a heart, a liver, and other organs, just as a human does. It has a long, strong backbone and a ribcage that helps protect the organs. Inside their fins, whales have long bones like fingers. All whales have blowholes to breathe through. Many toothed whales have dome-shaped foreheads called melons.

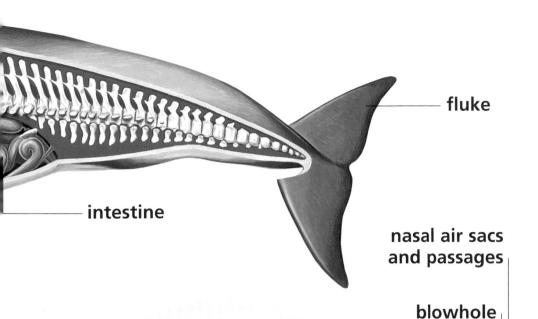

fluke

intestine

nasal air sacs
and passages

blowhole

melon

DID YOU KNOW?

Beluga whales make strange singing sounds. Scientists think these might be produced in the dome-shaped melon.

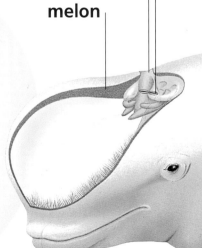

LARGE AND SMALL

A fully grown blue whale may be up to 98 feet
(30 meters) long and can weigh 165 tons (150 tonnes).
No animal on Earth is bigger than an adult blue

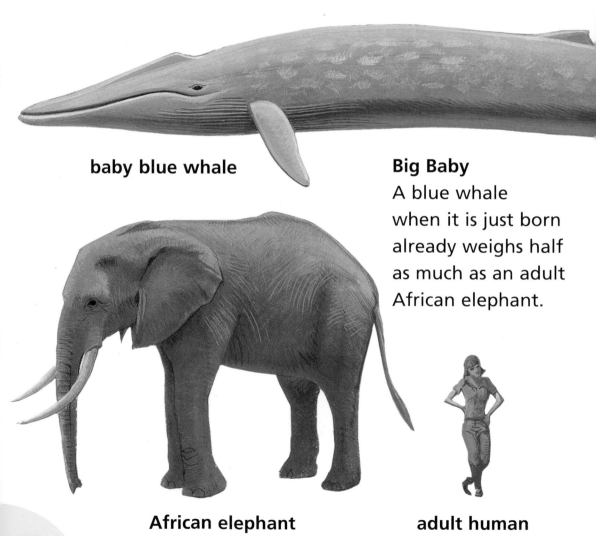

baby blue whale

Big Baby
A blue whale
when it is just born
already weighs half
as much as an adult
African elephant.

African elephant

adult human

whale. Most whales are bigger than other sea animals, but some are smaller than a shark. Some porpoises and dolphins are no larger than a human.

AMAZING!

A sperm whale has the largest brain of any animal. Its brain is about six times heavier than the average human brain.

Whales come in lots of different sizes, shapes, and colors. A blue whale grows to about five times the length of a beluga.

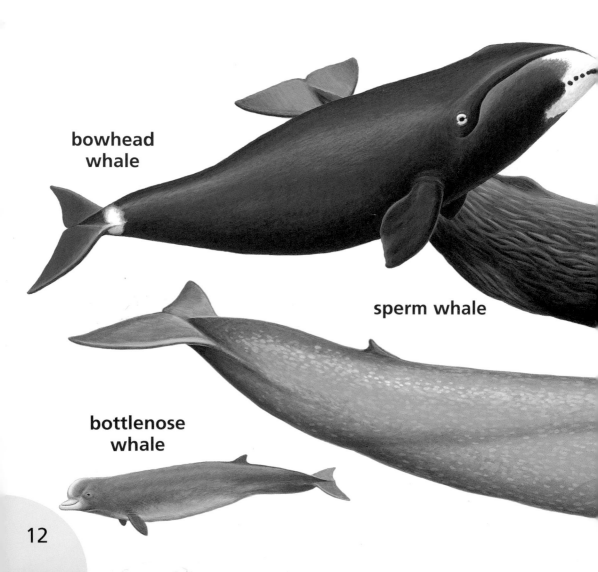

bowhead
whale

sperm whale

bottlenose
whale

gray whale

beluga

humpback whale

killer whale

blue whale

13

HEADS AND TEETH

Different whales have different-shaped heads and different teeth. Look at the whales below. The bottlenose dolphin has visible teeth in both jaws. The sperm whale's visible teeth are all in its lower jaw. The other two whales are baleen whales, so they have no teeth at all!

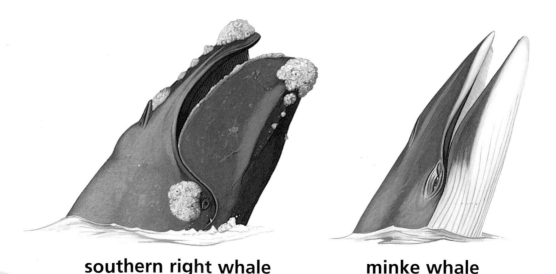

southern right whale   **minke whale**

DID YOU KNOW?

A male narwhal has one extra-long tooth that grows straight out of its upper jaw. This tusk can grow to over 7 feet (2 meters).

sperm whale   **bottlenose dolphin**

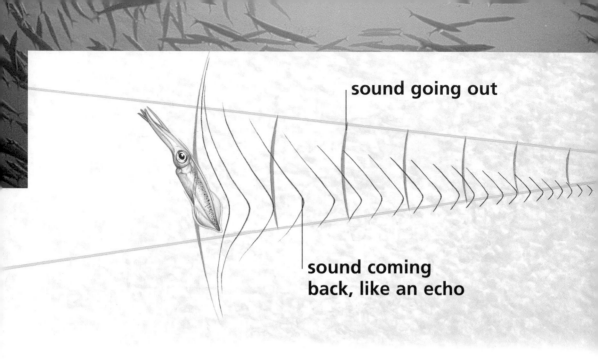

sound going out

sound coming
back, like an echo

LIVING IN THE DARK

Toothed whales hunt for food deep down in the sea
where it is dark. It is hard to see fish and other prey.
As it swims, the whale makes clicking noises. When
the noise hits a fish it bounces back like an echo,
so the whale knows where the fish is. This is
called echolocation.

DID YOU KNOW?

A bottlenose dolphin can use echolocation to find things 820 yards (750 meters) away.

FISHING FOR FOOD

Baleen whales are large, but they eat tiny fish and shrimp called krill. When a baleen whale finds a school of krill, it opens its jaws and swims toward it. Some baleen whales scoop up everything in their path. Others use the strands of baleen to strain the sea water and skim off the food. Many baleen whales feed near the surface of the ocean, but others dive down deep.

Diving for Food
A mass of tiny sea creatures flows into a humpback whale's mouth as it swims swiftly toward them.

A Bubble Net

Sometimes humpback whales trap their prey in a circle of bubbles blown through their blowhole. This bubble net makes the prey easy to catch.

Toothed whales usually eat their prey one at a time. They like large fish and other sea animals. Many toothed whales use their teeth to catch their food. Then they swallow it in one gulp, without chewing. Killer whales, or orcas, can even snatch seals from beaches or rocks that are just out of the water.

AMAZING!

The Ganges River dolphin uses one of its fins to stir up fish from the bottom of the river. Then it catches them in its long, narrow jaws.

Sperm Whale

Sperm whales will dive more than 1,300 feet (400 meters) in search of their favorite food, the giant squid.

sperm whale

bowhead whale

fin whale

Which Whale Is It?

You can tell many whales by the way they blow. The sperm whale is the easiest. It always blows forward and to the side.

BIG BLOW

Even though it lives in the sea, a whale still needs to breathe like any other mammal. Some whales can hold their breath under water for more than an hour. When a whale comes to the surface to breathe out, or blow, it sends a cloud of white vapor through its blowhole and high into the air. The blow from a large whale can be seen from far away.

humpback whale

Biggest Blow
The blue whale has the most powerful blow of all.

DOUBLE BLOWHOLE

Baleen whales, such as the humpback, have two blowholes. That is why their blow is so wide.

FINS AND FLUKES

A whale has two fins near the front of its body. It uses these pectoral fins, or flippers, to steer itself as it swims. At the end of its tail are two wide, flat flaps, called flukes. The whale moves these up and down to push itself forward through the water. Most whales also have a fin that stands up on their back. This is called a dorsal fin.

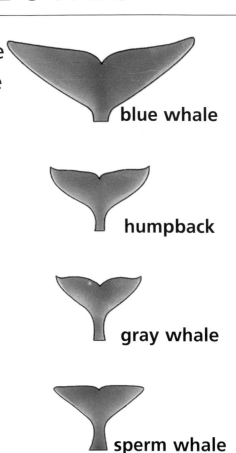

blue whale

humpback

gray whale

sperm whale

narwhal

Different Flukes
The biggest whales have the biggest flukes. They need lots of power to push themselves forward.

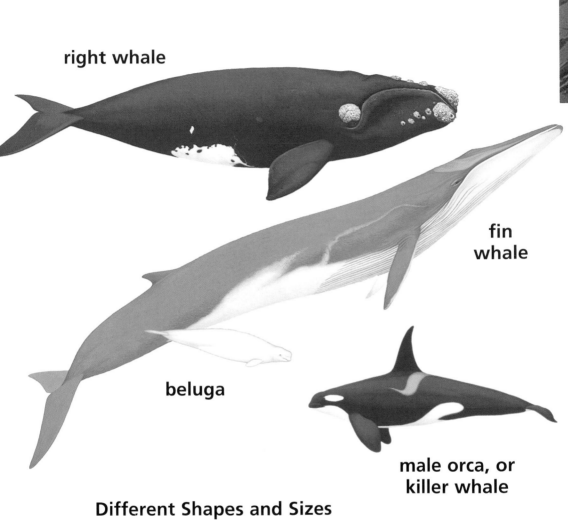

right whale

fin whale

beluga

male orca, or killer whale

Different Shapes and Sizes
Notice the shapes and sizes of different whales' fins. Right whales have no dorsal fin.

HIGH JUMPERS

Whales often hurl themselves high out of the water like huge acrobats. This is called breaching. Sometimes male whales breach when they are fighting. Other times they might breach to send messages to each other, or to get a clear view of people in boats. Sometimes they might do it just for fun.

High Jumper
A humpback makes a huge splash when it breaches. Whales sometimes breach like this many times in a row.

Pec-waving
A humpback often lies on its side and waves one of its pectoral fins in the air, slapping it hard against the water.

27

Keep Away

One reason that large whales wave their flukes is to warn other creatures to keep away. This means humans, too!

Safety in Numbers

Fraser's dolphins live in warm seas. They gather in groups of 100 or more.

Whales seem to enjoy each other's company, just like humans. Large groups of whales often feed or travel together. Groups of dolphins can sometimes be seen leaping out of the water one after the other as they swim past. Bottlenose dolphins are some of the easiest whales to watch because they usually live close to coastlines.

Forward Leaps
Dolphins take short leaps as they swim. This is called porpoising. It helps them move faster.

Leaps and Dives
Dusky dolphins can jump right out of the water, then dive back in head first.

29

GLOSSARY

baleen Long, strong strands that hang from the upper jaw of some whales. Whales that have baleen do not have teeth. Baleen is also known as whalebone.

esophagus A tube that leads from an animal's mouth to its stomach. Food passes through the esophagus.

intestines The long, winding tubes that food passes into when it leaves the stomach. These are also called bowels.

mammal An animal that grows inside its mother's body before it is born. The young drink their mother's milk.

prey Animals that are caught and eaten by other animals.

INDEX

CREDITS AND NOTES

Picture and Illustration Credits
[t=top, b=bottom, l=left, r=right, c=center, F=front, B=back, C=cover, bg=background]
Martin Camm 1c, 3tr, 7tc, 7bc, 14br, 14bl, 15bl, 15br, 16–17tc, 18–19bc, 19tr, 22tl, 22tc, 22tr, 23tl, 25c.
Corel Corporation 17bl, 23tr, 23br, 26lc, 27c, 28br, 29cr, 29bl, 30br, Cbg, 4–32 borders. **Chris Forsey** 15tl, FCt.
The Granger Collection, New York 5cl. **Gino Hasler** 4br, 6br, 6lc, 9br, BC, FClc. **David Kirshner** 8–9tc, 12–13c, 21c, FCbc. **Frank Knight** 2b, 10c, 10bc. **PhotoEssentials** 28tl.
Tony Pyrzakowski 4lc, 5c, 5tl, 11bc, 20lc, 24r, 31tr.

Acknowledgements
Weldon Owen would like to thank the following people for their assistance in the production of this book:
Jocelyne Best, Peta Gorman, Tracey Jackson, Andrew Kelly, Sarah Mattern, Emily Wood.